Peabody Girl Dog Gone Good

Book two of Tails of a Lady Dog Catcher

By

Nancy LeBaron-Kiley

Contents

Dedication

This book is dedicated to my crazy husband and best friend
Bart who has put up with my antics all of these years,
you're the best, love you.

About the Author

As a 19 year old animal lover, I was given the opportunity to become the first female Animal Control Officer, known back then as the Dog Catcher, in the U.S. and the youngest appointed municipal department head in the country: a record that the Guinness Book of Records feels cannot be broken and they are all about breaking records. I had the privilege of handling many different animals, some you would never expect to see in a small city in Massachusetts, but you will have to read my first book for those stories. I try to write my stories as if you were sitting in front of me and I was telling them to you, I hope I did a good job of that, but only you can answer that question. My stories, all true, are funny, some sad, and others hopefully elicit the fury in your heart that it did with me. I wanted justice for the animals I encountered. You, as a human, can always hire an attorney, but the animals only had me to represent them and get them justice for what was done to them. In today's world, animals have more advocates, and with social media, immediate response to their plight. Let's try to continue this trend and make it better day by day.

The Bat in the Bedroom

I was in my office at the Police Station when a call came in. I answered the phone to hear the voice of a very frantic girl yelling she had a bat in her bedroom and I had to come quickly. I calmed her down enough to give me a few details, like where she lived and headed that way. I figured this was a legitimate call because of her state of panic, which bats seem to elicit anytime they happen to come upon a human. You know the old wives tale; it will get caught in your hair, NOT. They have radar, and you aren't on it. Bats are a great thing to have around, not necessarily in your bedroom, but they consume a lot of mosquitoes and other flying insects that tend to bother people and usually only come out at dusk to feed. But with full bellies comes a nap. They tend to hang behind shutters on houses, chimneys, and other out-of-the-way places.

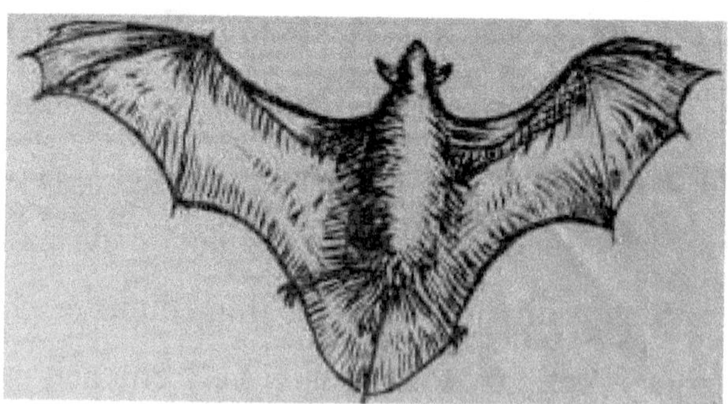

I got to her apartment on the second floor, and she let me in. She showed me to her bedroom door and then said, "Wait, I have to tell you something." Oh, this should be good. "I kind of freaked out and threw some clothes at it."

Okay, not a problem. I opened the door, you don't really think she was touching the door or going in, do you? Well, she most certainly did throw clothes at it. Hanging off the ceiling fan was a bra and a few socks, clothes everywhere, hanging off bureaus, closet doors, and bedposts. I think the whole wardrobe was thrown at this little guy. Now to the task of finding where he is hanging out. Every other second I heard, "Do you have him yet?" No, I'll let you know when I find him. After looking around for a few minutes, I found him hanging on the wall behind the bureau. I needed help moving it to reach behind and get him. Well, the only available body was Miss Frantic. It took me a few minutes to convince her that he wasn't going to attack her, he wasn't going to fly into her hair, and all the other reasons she could come up with not to go in the bedroom to help me move the bureau. I finally told her that if she didn't help me, she was on her own with Mr. Bat because I had other calls to make. How quickly she agreed to help. She only had to be in the room long enough to slowly move the bureau about 10 inches away from the wall. With the bureau moved, I could reach in and scoop him up. I always carried a hockey glove for handling little toothy creatures, especially toothy creatures that carry rabies. I gently got hold of him and made my way out of the bedroom. She had a porch off her kitchen, so I decided that was the fastest way to get him back into the real world he lived in. She was as far away from my friend and me the bat as she could possibly get, but as I got out onto the porch, she asked if she could see him before I released him. I told her that when I opened my gloved hand, he would probably fly off right away, but she was brave enough, out in the open anyways, to want to watch and see him. I slowly opened my hand, and he was just resting there. He looked at me, with no fear of me or anything, then he looked at her, opened his mouth to show her his teeth, hissed at her, and flew off. Now she is screaming, and I'm laughing, but she doesn't think this is funny at all. I figured I would have a little more fun and told her that he would be back at midnight! Her response was, "He will be alone. I'm moving out right now!" She went back inside and started packing her bags. She said she would hire someone to come in and move her stuff out because she was never setting foot in that apartment again.

Three inches of terror! Too funny in my thought process.

Ooo, Ooo, That Smell

I was sitting at my desk at the station when a call came in. It was the local hospital. They had a gentleman in the ER with his grandchild who was having seizures. When they questioned him about his grandson's medical history, he told them that he had just been bitten by his dog a few days previous to the seizures starting. They asked him if the dog was still at home. He nervously told them that the dog had died and was buried on his property. All the alarms were now going off. They needed that dog tested for rabies. I went to the gentleman's address to meet him and get the dog's body to bring to the vet to have the head removed because the state laboratory wants only the head of large animals. He had gone home from the hospital and immediately dug up the dog's remains, which he had buried in the pig dung! Did I fail to mention this was in the middle of the summer, and he was a pig farmer? Now you know the reason for the title of this chapter.

We loaded the dog's body into the van, a very big, long-haired German Shepherd covered in pig dung. I gave the Animal Hospital a heads-up on the situation (no pun intended) so that the Vet could come out to the van instead of bringing this odorous body into the hospital and causing a mass evacuation. He came out of the hospital with a saw. Yes, this sounds gross, but it's a fact of life. Now I have the head in a bag in the front seat with me and the body in the back as the Dr. at the hospital wants this rushed in, and the Vet Hospital doesn't want the body smelling up the place, so I'm left with getting rid of that too.

Let's start by saying I am not a Boston person. Put me in the woods, and I will find my way out, put me in Boston, and you may not see me for a few days. I get totally lost in all those ways. The station called the State Police to escort me in. I'm told to meet the trooper on the Tobin Bridge. He just gets ahead of me, no stopping. We are in a rush! Lights flashing, going fast, I don't know how we got there, but I think we broke a record.

We arrive at the State Lab; I grab the bag with the dog's head and rush inside to hand it over to the lab assistant. Sign all the paperwork, give all the information I have, and exit the building in about 15 minutes. The trooper was standing near his cruiser, so I walked over to thank him for his help. He looked at me like I was a giant cootie, pressed his back against the cruiser, and yelled, "DON'T TOUCH ME."   I'm thinking, what did I do? Then I got a whiff. OMG, that dog was really ripe. The trooper quickly inched his way sideways along the cruiser, back around to the driver's door, and took off. Oh great, I'm in Boston and just got left there by the trooper. I got some really nasty looks from people as I was trying to find my way out of Boston, and no one got or stayed too close to the van for any length of time. It was really kind of embarrassing to be driving with that odor; there was a cloud of smell following me down the road. It took me a while to get back but then I had to dispose of the body, naturally in the local landfill or dump as we affectionately called it. The dump guys weren't too happy with me either. One actually lost his lunch and called me a few names. Hey, not my fault!

Well, a few weeks later, another call came in. This time a little girl found an injured rat on her lawn. She wanted to help it and picked it up, yep, it bit her and then died. Here we go again. At least this rat didn't smell or need its head taken off. We put the rat in a baggie, and the station called the Boston Police this time to meet me on the Tobin Bridge. I think the State Police had labeled a call for help for me as offensive. Anyway, I arrive at the Tobin Bridge, and there is the Boston Police cruiser waiting. He pulls in front of me, puts on his blue lights, and we are speeding through traffic. What is going on? This is really not a situation we need to go fast for. We get to the State Lab in record time again. We stop at the door, and the two officers get out of the cruiser. I get out of my Dog Officer van, clearly marked as such, and they shout, "WHERE IS SHE?" "Where is who, I ask?" "The little girl bitten by the rat!" they reply.   I look at them, lift up my baggie with the rat in it and say, "I have the rat!"   Really, I am not an ambulance. The look on their faces was priceless. We were booking around corners on two wheels at about 60 mph for a rat! I doubt very much that they ever told their coworkers that story in its full context.

Bulls on the Highway

So imagine driving down the highway behind a livestock trailer, the door swinging open, and two large trash bags falling out, only they weren't trash bags. They were Black Angus cows. That is what the reporting person told the State Police dispatcher. I was out in my van when the control room called me on my radio, 5225 (my code name), report of two loose bulls between Rtes 1 and I-95, State Police on the scene need your assistance. Now the area is not in Peabody but in the neighboring town of Danvers, which does not have an animal control person. The area I think I need to get to is accessible by going down Rte. 1, going around and over 95, and then taking the ramp to get onto 95. Well, I get to the area and find the State Police standing on Rte 1, flagging me down. I pulled over, got out of the van, and was informed that a person traveling down I-95 with a trailer and two cows in it had lost its load on 95 and that the cows were now in the bushes between Rte 1 and I-95. The State Police were searching for the vehicle in question, who obviously didn't know he had lost something. I know nothing about cows except their strength. I need to call in a vet for help on this one. I call my equine vet, Dr. Minster, who knows how to handle cows.

While we wait for him to arrive, I get out the tranquilizer gun for him to use if needed and then go on a search for where exactly the cows are hiding out. Seems the bigger one has decided to take a rest from the ordeal it has just been through while the smaller one is roaming around in the bushes, maybe looking for the bigger one, who knows? Dr. Minster arrives at about the same time the State Police arrive with the owner of the trailer they fell out of. We find out that the bigger cow is blind and a female while the smaller one is her son, yes, a baby bull, oh joy. We tried getting mum to her feet, but nope, she was not moving. Dr. Minster puts a halter and lead rope on the cow and tells everyone to step back. He walks over to the side of the cow, cups his hand over her ears, and screams YAH!

The cow jumps to her feet and freezes.

WOW, I'm impressed. I'll have to remember that trick, never know when it might come in handy. We get the trailer open and load the cow in. Now for junior! He wasn't going to be as easy. He was a little frantic, calling for his mum, who was ignoring him as all mother cows do.

Dr. Minster loaded the tranquilizer into the dart and loaded the gun. He got him on the first shot, good job. Took a couple of minutes to take effect, but the bull went down on the top of a steep slope next to a drainage culvert on the I-95 side of the highway.

Myself, Dr. Minster, two State Troopers were charged with the task of dragging him down to the trailer, which was now on the side of the highway waiting for us.

Dragging the bull down the slope was going well until I fell into a hole next to the culvert, and the bull landed on me. This can only happen to me! We maneuvered the bull so I could escape and continued down the slope. Did I happen to mention that this was a very hot and humid day? We were all dripping wet and exhausted. We finally got the bull to the trailer; the owner opened the door and decided to put the now sleeping bull on the floor in the same space as mum. I may not know anything about cows, but I do know that a blind animal that feels something against its legs is not going to be happy about it. I told the owner it was not a good idea and that mum was going to kick the crap out of this sleeping bull. He didn't want to hear it, and they packed the bull in. Sure enough, mum started kicking at the thing by her feet. I screamed at the guy and grabbed the bull's legs to pull him back out. The owner gets in my face! As I was about to cold cock this guy, one of the troopers grabbed me and moved me away from him while the other trooper told this jerk to behave or be arrested for various offenses. What got me really angry was he had secured his broken trailer door with a coat hanger.

Really????? This idiot doesn't know anything about animal safety and shouldn't be allowed to go on his way. One of the troopers found something stronger in his trunk to secure the door, and off the idiot went. Both troopers, at this point, were exhausted and showing signs of heat stroke. One sat on the edge of his open trunk and fell backward into it. We had to get him some water to cool him down and revive him. Luckily Dr. Minster was always prepared and had some with him. This is really not the end of the story because we all were running through the shrubs and didn't notice the poison ivy. Yep, we all got it. It was like a never-ending story.

Farnsy Ferret Mouse

One of the places I had my horses was at the local veterinarians' hospital. He had a barn he wasn't using, and he allowed me to keep my horses there as long as I took care of his horse too. No problem, mucking stalls is therapeutic for me. Been doing it all my life. So one day, I got to the barn and found a ferret in a cage in the basement attached to the barn. It was a garage on the upper-level basement on the lower level attached to the barn to give you an idea of the layout. I went over to see the little guy, he seemed friendly, but I always had a healthy respect for animals I don't know anything about. I took a walk up to the animal hospital to find out about him. The Dr. told me that the ferret, which he called Fred, was found by Fish and Wildlife officers in a dumpster, abandoned. Ferrets at the time were illegal to own in Massachusetts. The Dr. had a permit that allowed him to keep him, but it seemed Fred was a troublemaker. They had him in the animal hospital and would let him out of his cage to roam around and get some exercise, but being a ferret. could open up drawers and cabinets and do what ferrets do best, ferret around for things. He got banished from the animal hospital when he gnawed all the earbuds off the stethoscopes; every stethoscope he could find, along with assorted other things to his liking. After about a week of seeing him all alone in a cage in the basement, I decided to kidnap him. I took him home and renamed him Farnsworth the Ferret Mouse, AKA Farnsy. He was so sweet and playful and loved being a snoop and getting into trouble. I had a front entryway, no heat, just a few windows, and a doorway we never used. This room also had French doors to enter the main house. It was a perfect place to make a home for him. I got a cardboard box and put a towel in it for him. I put down some cat litter, and we started our adventure of having a house ferret. If you have never had the pleasure of owning a ferret, they are the epitome of comedy.

He got into so much trouble!

First on his agenda was to make himself the home he wanted. He would wait for laundry day, and he started his hoarding of socks and any other soft material he could find. It was funny watching his eyes light up when he found a pair of my husband's underwear.

He would have it hanging out of the side of his mouth as he ran through the house on the way to his room and his box to stash it. Even funnier was watching my husband chasing him and yelling, "Give me back my coo covers!"

I remember coming home from work one day, and I couldn't find him. Not in his room or box, hunted around everywhere. I never thought the little troublemaker would go up the stairs. I went up, looking around. We have a pedestal bed with drawers underneath. I found one of the drawers quarter ways open, thought, I don't remember going in there this morning, so I closed it.

Well, almost, it wouldn't close, and I heard a squeaky scream. I took the drawer out, and sure enough, there he was. He had taken all of my socks and pulled them behind the partially opened drawer, and made himself another bed to sleep in. Took him downstairs, and from that time on, we had to put a piece of plywood across the stairs to keep him from going up and getting into trouble.

He didn't care; there was plenty of trouble to get into downstairs. He would lie on the floor and stretch out, a perfect opportunity for the cat to come and sit on him. Farnsy didn't like being sat on, so he would turn and bite the cat's belly, the cat would hiss and whack him, and then the chase was on. Across the living room, up the couch, down the couch, the cat was trying to get away from this little monster who just bit his belly.

Now Farnsy would go through all the natural states that a ferret in the wild would go through because his room was not heated.

In the summer, he would get slim and turn brown. In the winter, when it was cold, he would fatten up and turn white which was warmth and disguise from predators. I had bought a key chain for my husband to put in his Christmas stocking that was a bug that made noise when you pushed the button. It was kind of a BZZZ, BZZZ, BZZZ sound, and it flashed green. I had been watering my indoor plants and putting the empty watering can down on the floor. Farnsy decided to investigate. He knocked it over and had to squeeze his fat little body into it.

My husband thought it would be funny to throw the bug keychain in there with him. So you heard this faint buzzing coming from the plastic watering can, and Farnsy wanted no part of it, problem was he was so fat that the watering can got stuck on his butt. Here he is, running around in circles trying to get away from this thing inside the watering can that is, in his mind, going to eat him. We were in tears laughing. This went on for a good minute or two until he was finally able to free himself.

He turned on the watering can, growled at it, and ran for his room. He would avoid contact with that watering can forever after that. Just the sight of it sent him running.

At house parties, Farnsy always managed to scare someone. He loved climbing up and into the sleeves of nice warm jackets and coats to sleep.

Imagine sticking your arm in a sleeve and having it come to life. We never knew where he would pop up, which made having him so much fun.

Farnsy still belonged to Fish and Wildlife, and occasionally they would come and get him to take him to schools to show the kids about wildlife. I had trained him to wear a harness, and we would go for walks. He would stop traffic when we would take a walk in the grass at the school across the street from my house. All you saw was this bouncing thing on a leash. They don't walk, they bounce.

One day I came home to find Farnsy lying on the couch, not moving. A not moving ferret is cause for concern. I grabbed him up, and off to the vet, we went. The vet explained to me that ferrets are notorious tumor factories, and he was showing signs of that. I had to humanely euthanize Farnsy as the vet was sure he had a tumor. I wanted to know. I had him do a necropsy on him right then and there with me present.

Farnsy had a small tumor, but that is not what got him. He had a hernia that had ruptured, and he was septic, which means the infection from the hernia had made its way throughout his system, and it was shutting down.

That little ferret gave me more smiles and giggles. One day I will have another, my only hope being he is as personable as Farnsy was. I had him cremated, and he is residing in a special place with two other of my pets.

Quack

I decided one day to take my dog for a walk.

Nice spring sunny day, not too warm, just a comfortable sunny day. I thought it would be nice to take a different route than we normally took and headed toward the center of town. We crossed over to Elm and then onto Sylvan St., where the big library sits.

Behind the library is a nice little pond where people can sit and watch the geese, ducks, swans, and herons hang out.

It's not a very deep pond, and occasionally you see kids fishing. Now I know there are snapping turtles in this pond because I've had to rescue a few females making their way across the street to the cemetery to lay eggs. In case you didn't know, only females cross the streets. Males just stay in the pond, eating and having a good time during the breeding season.

We were walking along beside the pond when I noticed a white duck limping and being attacked by the other ducks, yes, breeding season. When you rescue animals for a living is a never-ending job. I had to help this poor duck. White ducks are usually kept as pets or for food, so seeing a white duck amongst the wild ducks concerned me too. Tied the dog to the guardrail and jumped over it. The pond had a slope that was rock covered, and the duck had managed to get up out of the water and onto the rocks. She tried to get away, but with her injured leg, she just sort of rolled down the rocky slope and back into the water, where the attack started again, and she was struggling. Off came the sneakers, and in I went. It wasn't deep where she was, and I managed to get a hold of her. She didn't fight me at all, and I think she was relieved to get away from the barrage of boys that were after her. Well, I looked her over, her general feathers and wings looked okay, but her foot was all swollen. A decision was made; the duck needed to see the vet. Remember I said I was walking the dog? Now I'm walking the dog, and I have a duck tucked up under the other arm. I got a lot of attention walking through the center of town. I'm laughing to myself, thinking these people are probably wondering what this nut is doing walking a dog with a duck in her arms. Cruiser goes by, and I just see the officer shaking his head. He could have offered a ride!

I got home with the duck and called the vet.

He was there, and I could go right up.

It also helps that he was where I had my "dog pound" at the time. I go through the back door and into the exam area. The vet starts taking a look and tells me that the duck has "bumblefoot."

What the hell is bumblefoot?

Seems bumblefoot is an infection that starts in the bottom of the duck's foot caused by sharp rocks, sticks, etc.

Once the duck (or any bird) gets this, the infection can be treated, it's expensive, I'm told by the vet, but the foot will probably never be the same again. It will still be swollen and funny looking compared to the bird's normal foot.

He suggests I just put it back in the pond. I have the picture of those rotten boys attacking her in my brain, nope, I'll find another pond.

I take the duck home with me. Now, what do I do? I don't want to keep her in a crate while I make some phone calls, so I decided to put some water in the bathtub and put her in there. Only one problem, I forgot to pull the shower curtain closed, but I did close the door. I'm sitting and looking through my contacts to see who has a pond and might want to let the duck reside there. While I'm doing this, my husband comes home. He says, "Ah, Nancy, why is there water coming out from under the bathroom door?" I look and start laughing. Oh, oh. I open the door, and the duck is having the time of her life, splashing the water all over her and all over the bathroom. I now have a roll of soaking wet toilet paper, and the curtains on the window are drenched. I mean, this duck was a busy girl and could make that water fly!

I have to explain to my husband that she is injured and has seen the vet, and I'm trying to find a different spot for her, don't worry. I'll clean up the mess. He remembered a job he did in Boxford, and the woman had a pond in her backyard. Perfect.

He gave her a call and said we could bring the duck to her pond. It was a small pond but fine for Mrs. Duck. There were a couple of geese but no other ducks. When we left, she was swimming around and seemed quite content. This was not a wild duck and should be able to fly. I just hope she doesn't fly back to Danvers. About three weeks later, I called to find out how the duck was doing and got some sad news. It seems being lame that she wasn't able to escape a raccoon on the prowl. At least I tried.

Squealing Pig

I had a call from my local Fish and Wildlife officer asking if he could meet up with me about a problem he was investigating in Peabody. This officer was a friend of mine, and he was in charge of the district Peabody was in: his name is Bill, and if you read my first book, you met Bill. He likes to get me in trouble like I need help! Bill explained to me that they were contacted by the State Health Department, and it seems that they had three cases of trichinosis in Peabody, and all three folks had eaten at the same church cookout where pork was served. Trichinosis is a food-borne microscopic parasite. People can get this parasite by eating undercooked meats from animals infected with it, such as bears or pork. Bill had the name of the pig farm in Peabody that the pig came from. If you are going to roast a whole pig, it is a very long cooking process. I mean hours upon hours of a pig on a spit to cook all the way through. I don't know who the cook was, but obviously, the pig was not cooked properly or thoroughly.

We weren't concerned about the chef, only where the pig came from. We headed out in Bill's truck to go talk to the pig farmer and let him know we needed one of his pigs for testing. When we got close to his farm, I knew where we were going because the pig farms in the area were off 128, one on the North side of the highway and two on the south side, and in the summertime, when you passed that area, the smell would curl your hair. We parked on the road and would have to walk into his pig farm, which was in the woods.

I knew this farmer; he had his pigs on a piece of property that he rented, no house, just out in the woods.

He was right down the road from another pig farmer that I had had a cruelty case for not getting vet care for a pig with a broken leg. The Health Dept was in charge of sanitary conditions on pig farms, but they certainly didn't do anything about these guys, or maybe they didn't know they even had this place. When you feed pigs, garbage, it has to be cooked. Fresh vegetables and bread didn't have to be cooked, but food thrown out by the local restaurants had to be cooked down. How yummy is that!

We walked down the dirt road to the "farm," trash was strewn everywhere, old tires and old barrels where supposedly he was cooking the garbage he fed the pigs.

Feel like having a pork chop yet? If you had seen all of the property, you would never eat pork again! So Bill is looking around and calling for the owner, and I hear a kitten crying. Oh no, here we go. I follow the sound and come upon a six-week-old (estimated) kitten with its head caught between an old tire and a rock. I freed the kitten, and as I was walking away, she ran up the back of my leg and got on my shoulder. No, no, little kitty, I'm busy, I can't pay you any attention at the moment, and I put her back on the ground. She's not it, and back up my leg, she climbs and onto my shoulder. Okay, you can come for the ride. Here I am, walking around the pig "farm" with a kitten sleeping on my shoulder. I spot Bill, and I get this dirty look. Hey, not my fault the kitten found a spot to sleep. It seems there is no one on the property except us, so we continue to look around.

He had found a sow with a bunch of young pigs.

He decides a young one is just what we need to have tested. If you have never grabbed a baby pig before, it's exciting, to say the least. The minute we put our hands on it the pig started screaming and never stopped. He hands me the baby pig and says run. I still have a kitten on my shoulder, too, quite the trio, me running, pig squealing, and the kitten sleeping. Obviously, we didn't count on this scenario. We get to his truck, and we all hop in. I hadn't noticed that the little pig had crapped all over my uniform.

It looked like mustard and had the worst smell ever, obviously, in my mind anyways, from what it had been eating.

Bill is trying to drive and keep from throwing up, and I am sitting there looking down at the mess that is all over the front of my uniform and a still squealing pig. Now my brain goes to who I can chase down for a hug with all the pig crap on me, but the smell was starting to get to me too, so I canned the idea of heading back to the station for some fun. I'll take a skunk smell any day over this. We headed back to where I had parked my van. I give Bill a small crate to put the still-screaming pig in, and I am left with a sleeping kitten on my shoulder and a foul-smelling shirt. I head home to clean up and drop the kitten off at my house.

A couple of days later, Bill shows up at the barn where I keep my horse and says he has my crate for me. He tells me he will leave it by my truck. He doesn't tell me that he also left me with the young pig. I called him. He says the pig tested negative, and I was now the owner of a pig. How did this happen? He figured I had an extra stall at the barn, and I could raise it for food. I already have a kitten at home from this pig "farm," and now I have the pig. Do you know that pigs poop very similar to people? I don't deal well with people poop. I got this pig to a good weight as fast as I could and then took him to the butcher.

Never again will I raise a pig! I had to throw my uniform shirt out, and it took a good three days for the smell to leave my nostrils and skin. As for the kitten, she lived to be 19 years old, and that is an astonishing age for a cat, but she was as nutty as they come.

I would put my foot under her butt and tell her to burn rubber, and she would scream and kick off my foot running. She was something. Great cat and a lot of fun. Still have her ashes. RIP Bushky.

Portuguese Bang Bang

One of my calls came from an older Portuguese gentleman who raised rabbits.

Seems some of the neighborhood dogs were coming in and harassing and taking his rabbits. In Massachusetts, if you raise animals for food and a dog is chasing or killing your livestock (it has to be edible livestock, horses aren't edible), you have a right to shoot the dog, but you have to make sure it is not wounded but dead, otherwise, you can be charged with cruelty. He told me what the dogs looked like, and he gave me some names of the people he thought might own them. Before I talk to anyone about a problem dog, I always check on two things, a rabies certificate and license. I can now go check to see if they indeed have these dogs. The first person I went to see didn't own any dogs, but his next-door neighbor did, and he let them run loose. Sounds like I have my dogs. I went next door and knocked on the door. No barking dogs, probably because they are out running the neighborhood.

The gentleman answers and starts telling me they aren't his. He doesn't know who they belong to, yadda, yadda, yadda.

Do I believe him? NO. So I said ok, once I shoot them, I'm sure the owner will show up for the bodies. The guy goes ballistic. You can't shoot dogs!!! Oh yes, I can, especially if they are killing livestock. It's the law. So I ask him why he's so upset about it if they aren't his dogs. I love putting liars over a barrel. He now confesses they are his dogs, but he didn't know that they were killing livestock.

LIAR, the dogs probably brought one of their kills home. Yep, they did, but he thought they were wild rabbits. So now I asked if he had rabies certificates and licenses on the dogs.

Oh yes, he says. Here comes the barrel again. So I tell him that when I get back to the station, I am going to check this out, and if he is lying to me, he is really going to be in a heap of trouble.

He confesses again to not having either.

I explained to him how much I could fine him for no rabies shots, then how much I could fine him going all the way back to April 1st, per day, per dog @ $25. You could see the math calculator going off in his head. He wants to make a deal. I told him he was to go see the owner of the rabbits and make restitution for the damage his dogs had done, and if he didn't, I would get a court summons on him. He then was to get his dogs to a veterinarian for rabies shots and then take those certificates to City Hall and get them licensed. I told him I wanted to know what veterinarian he was going to because I was going to check up on him, and he did give me the name and the date of his appointment. A couple of days after my encounter with the dog owner, I went to see the rabbit guy to see if the dog owner had made contact with him. He was all excited to see me and thanked me. The dog owner had come by and paid him for his lost rabbits and was promised he wouldn't ever see them again.

He thought I was the best. He then says to me, "Come down into my basement. I want you to have something." I politely say no thank you, but he won't hear of it. Ok, down into a dark basement, I go. He has a bottle for me, clear liquid with no label. Now I have only heard about Bang Bang and never tasted it, but it's basically Portuguese moonshine. He wants to give me a cup, and I tell him no, I'm on duty, and I don't drink. He wants to give me a bottle of it. No, thank you, I don't drink. I'm not touching that stuff. I've heard too many stories about it. He doesn't like the fact that he can't give me something for helping him. I told him it was my job and not to worry about it. I finally get out of the basement and am on my way. But he wants to pay me for helping him. Several days later, he shows up at the Police Station. I get a call to come to the station that a gentleman is waiting to see me in the vestibule. I go in, and there is my friend, the rabbit guy. He has a plate of fried rabbit for me. Now I like rabbit both live and cooked and decide to take this because I don't know what he will think of next. It does look really good, and look a lot like chicken drumsticks. I was walking through the station, asking anyone if they wanted to try some. Wow, I didn't know I worked with a bunch of sissies, all afraid to eat rabbit. I was walking down the hall, and here comes the Chief.

I'm not asking him if he wants any. He raises rabbits as pets. He sees the dish and grabs one as he walks by. Oh Oh! I turned and yelled, "Chief, that's bunny!" He turned so fast I never saw the bunny leg coming my way, and it hit me square in the forehead. Then he yells at me, "You're a sick person!" I tried to explain that I didn't slaughter or kill the bunnies, but he was not talking to me or listening to anything I had to say. He kicked me out of the station AGAIN. Normally I only get kicked out for snakes, not bunnies.

The Dangerous Dog

I had been getting calls from a lot of folks who lived in this one neighborhood about a husky that belonged to an older couple who lived on the street. Seems this husky didn't like people and would scare and chase the kids on their way to school. I went to the house, and an older woman came to the door. This was about 9:00 a.m. I explained to her that I was having complaints about her dog. She said he only got out once in a great while, and she would take care of the situation. I asked if he was licensed, and she said he was. Okay, I'll check this out when I get back to the station.

The dog was licensed.

Several weeks later, I got a call from another neighbor. The dog is loose and chasing people. I head down again. I can't find this dog. I patrol around for a bit and then leave. A couple of days later, the same thing happened, a different caller. I go back, but I still don't see any husky. The folks on the street had had enough and called their ward councilor about the problem. Now City Hall is involved. I explained that I had gone there on every call but hadn't seen the dog out. Under the law, a complaint can be made to the Chief of Police regarding dangerous dogs. The folks on the street filed a complaint. The Chief called me in to discuss the problem. He scheduled a meeting with the owners of the dog and with the neighbors. He told the

Husky owners they had to get the dog out of Peabody. He deemed the dog a nuisance. They weren't much affected by his ruling, which I thought strange. I would fight for my dog! About three weeks went by, and the neighbors called. The husky was still there and was running loose again. He had ripped a backpack of a kid heading to school. His mother was furious, and I couldn't blame her. I took out a court summons on them to take the dog away from them as they had not complied with the order from the Chief. While waiting for this court date, I got additional information about the owners. It seems that it was an older married couple. I also learned that they were alcoholics, but they drank Vanilla Extract, not booze. I had never heard of this but then was told by one of the patrolmen who knew them that they would have a case of vanilla extract delivered every week and that Vanilla extract had a higher alcohol level than a lot of liquors. I also found out that they kept this poor dog chained to a lally column in the basement and that they were scared to death of this dog. That doesn't explain to me how it keeps getting out if it's chained and they are afraid of it. I feel bad for the dog, but now I have some ammunition to use in court.

The court date comes. I am sitting in the courtroom along with probation officers, police officers, state troopers, and court officers, and there they are, hammered on vanilla extract and crying. One of the probation officers comes over to me and says, "How can you be so heartless that you want to take their dog away from them?" Excuse me?? You don't know the story. The judge listened, but he is an animal lover, to his credit, but in this circumstance, he needs to listen to the facts. Doesn't matter, crocodile tears and the fact that they are close to 70 years old and I'm the mean one. Judge tells them they can keep their dog, but it has to remain under constant restraint, and if it gets loose again, the Police can shoot it. I still feel bad for the dog. Who knows what they are doing to this poor dog while being hammered and causing the dog to be vicious? It didn't take long. Got a call about 7:30 a.m. about three weeks later that the dog was loose, and parents were furious. Chief hears the call and sends me and a cruiser to the neighborhood. A few people come out and say the dog is still out and about. I went to the owner's house. The dog is on the front porch, not tied. We yell to the woman who comes to the door. She is belligerent, already drinking and drunk, giving us a hard time.

She slams the door. A few seconds later, she opens the door and comes out onto the porch with the dog. We tell her to take him by the collar and bring him in. She starts crying. She can't. She doesn't want him to bite her again.

She goes back into the house and leaves the dog on the porch. The door opens again. She is back to being belligerent. We tell her that if the dog comes off the porch, the patrolman is going to shoot him. She goes back into the house, leaving the dog on the porch again. The door opens a few seconds later, and she is crying again and pleading not to shoot her dog. We tell her again, take him into the house. She slams the door. Now the dog comes down the steps and takes off running. The patrolman gets out the shotgun, and the hunt starts. I am walking up the street, looking into the yards that aren't fenced. Luckily I am close to the cruiser, and his windows are down. All of a sudden, the patrolman yells, "Nancy, jump through the window of the cruiser NOW!" The husky had come up from behind me and was in a stalking position. Paul, the patrolman, came running as I launched myself into the front seat of the cruiser. The dog took off into someone's yard, and I heard the shot. The dog was dead. I felt bad that the dog had lived such a rotten life with these drunks, but in the end, he was now hopefully in a happier place, and the abuse was over.

Dogs are not born vicious; it is the owners who make them that way.

Harvey

This story is about what I just spoke about, people trying to make dogs into mean, aggressive dogs. There are some who don't become vicious but are scared and shy.

This story is about Harvey, the pit bull.

Got a call from a woman who told me she opened the door to get her mail, and a dog ran into her house and was hiding behind her couch. I asked her if she knew what kind of dog it was, but she said she was afraid to go look. She had never seen him in her area before. She lived on a main drag between Peabody, Salem, and Danvers, so he could have come from anywhere.

I took a ride to her house, and she invited me in.

We were in her side porch area, where she had her TV and a couch. She told me that this was the couch he was hiding behind. I didn't hear any growling or whimpering, but when I peeked over the top of the couch, I saw a stocky pit bull with a spiked collar on, and he had his head down, cowering. So someone is trying to make this dog vicious, was my first thought.

You don't put a collar like that on a poodle or lab or any dog with a reputation for having a gentle disposition.

I talked to the dog for a bit, but he just sat there hanging his head and not really reacting to me. I got the obvious signs that he was handled by a man.

Most dogs hear a woman's voice and immediately think of food, as most dogs are fed by the woman of the house, but he is so scared he doesn't move.

I moved the couch away from the wall, far enough for me to be able to sit at the end of the couch away from him, and let him make the decision to approach. I also turned my back to him, showing submission. It probably took about 15 minutes and a few encouraging cookies tossed his way, but he decided I was probably okay. I felt a cold nose on my neck, then a gentle nose push under my arm, and there you have it. We were friends. He was a sweetheart but a scared little guy. He wasn't showing any of the severe traumatic signs like shaking or trying to run and hide, so that was a plus for me. I sat on the floor for about 15 minutes with him, patting him and talking to him. I am a firm believer that if you talk to an animal, they listen and understand more than you think. I told him I was going to put a leash on him and that we would be taking a ride. He was very calm and let me put the leash around his neck. I gave him another cookie and told him what a good boy he was. I got up slowly so as not to scare him, and he seemed fine with that.

This collar was killing me. Ever put your arm around a dog's neck and get spiked? I had no choice; my first priority was gaining his trust.

I loaded him up in the front seat of my van, where he could be near me, and we took off for the vet. I'll have him checked out, get that collar off him and then get him in a cage with some food and water. He was in good health, and the girls at the vet clinic loved him, and he loved them back.

He really was a love bug and couldn't get enough attention. I went to the local pet store and bought him a normal collar, and ditched the spiked one.

If anyone claimed him, I would just tell them he didn't have a collar on when I found him. The vet clinic was also where I had my barn and horses. I would go every day and pick up Harvey to go for rides with me while on patrol. Harvey was a great dog, very gentle, and never made a wrong move toward my horses or anyone he met. The problem was the pit bull's reputation. He really did not deserve to be labeled a pit bull. He was way too sweet for that moniker. By law, I am only allowed to keep dogs for ten days, and in that time, I need to find a home or, at the end of that time frame, euthanize the dog. I always, with every dog, made up a new slip on them, changed the color, sex, or whatever it took to keep them another ten days so I could try to round up a home.

I found a lot of homes for dogs doing this, but there were some that were not so lucky. I managed to find Harvey a home. The people who adopted him sent me letters about how loving he was, and they were so glad to have a dog like him. Sometimes I would get a dog returned for various reasons. I don't know their past, and some turned out to be trash pickers, not housebroken or house wreckers eating couches and other furniture. Those were the unlucky ones. No one would take a dog with any of those problems. When they were returned for one of these problems they were humanely euthanized. The worst part of my job, but at least I tried to give them a chance at a good life.

Lady, I'm Not a Vet

Had a call come through the control room about a woman concerned about her dog. I had no information other than something was wrong, and she wanted to talk to me. I called her back, and she was quite upset.

Seems her dog wasn't eating, and she wanted me to come and look at him. I told her that I was not a veterinarian and she should take her dog to her vet. She is crying. No one is home to help her; she doesn't want anything to happen to him while she waits for someone to come home and help her, and the story and tears continue. I finally agreed to come and make sure her dog was okay until someone came home to help her get the dog to the vet.

I get to her house, and she points me toward a door to the basement. She tells me he is down there. I ask her how long ago he ate; she tells me that he hasn't eaten since yesterday.

Okay, it could be a stomach bug, I'm thinking, or it could be something worse like an impaction. I went down the stairs slowly as I didn't know this dog and forgot to ask what kind of dog it was. I get to the bottom of the stairs, and I see a dog lying there. I start talking to it as I approach so as not to alarm the dog; it's a really big shepherd. He doesn't move. I get closer. Now I see the dog's lifeless eyes. I touch him. He is as stiff as a board, which means he has been lying here dead for some time. I walked back up the stairs and said, "Your dog is dead, how long has he been there?"

She told me he had died several days ago, but she didn't know what to do with him, so she waited and called me. He had died over the weekend, and this was now Monday. She said she wanted me to take his body. "Nope."

"Your dog, your problem." Take him to your vet and have him disposed of. Now she starts getting nasty. I'm a taxpayer, and I want you to take the dog to the dump. "Nope."

She was now seething and calling me names. I just walked away, got back in my van, and went to the station to make out a report. I knew this was not the end of this nasty ass lady.

I was right! She called her City Councilor, the Mayor, the Police Chief, and everyone she could think of.

They all agreed that this dog was in her house and her problem. I don't know who told her that, but she took it one step further. She wrapped the dog's body in an old rug and put it out on the sidewalk. This is in the summertime, by the way, nice and warm. She called her Councilor back and told him it was now the City's problem. It was out on the curb on the side of the street. The Councilor called me, NO, I am not picking up her dead dog. I told him that I had found out she had a 20-year-old son who could dispose of the body. She wasn't having her son do it, the City should do it. The dog has been dead for almost a week and is sitting out on the side of the street, rotting, smelling, and the herd of flies flying around the dead body wrapped in an old rug is getting out of control. Now the neighbors are getting involved calling everyone to get rid of this problem. I stood my ground. I'm a female and not strong enough to lift a large dead dog wrapped in a rug. My strategy worked. The city officials were now trying to figure out how to get this taken care of. They send down a crew from the Public Works Dept. The two guys got out of the truck, approached the rug, and both ended up throwing up right there in the street. They left without the body. They also refused to touch it because it was covered in maggots. This was really starting to get out of hand. They stopped calling me, thankfully. The trashmen also refused to pick it up on trash day. This woman was fighting with all the neighbors and trying to blame me. A few called, and I explained the situation to them, and then they got the whole story, but that didn't solve the problem. The City finally got one of the City Mechanics, who had a hydraulic lift on the back of his truck, to go pick it up and take it to the dump. This poor man was in his 60's and didn't need this added to his daily tasks, but he had been told the story, understood my position and went with gloves and his hydraulic lift pick-up to get the body. He didn't fare that well either. He got sick from the smell, but being an older person who had been around things like this before, he pushed through and dragged the rug onto his hydraulic lift, and set out for the dump. I heard about this and went to see him the following day. I explained the whole situation to him and apologized that he had been sent instead of some young guys. He was such a gentleman and told me not to worry; he felt bad that they were trying to get me to do this all alone and without the proper equipment.

My evil side wanted someone to do the same to her when she died, but there are laws against that. DAM!

Podengo Dogs

I really don't remember how I got this call, but I was sent to call for a bag floating in a small brook on the city line between Salem and Peabody. The caller could hear puppies crying. I got there as fast as I could and retrieved a bag of four puppies, two were already dead, but I had two to try to save. The water was cold, and the puppies were soaked, so I ran back to my Mum's house.

She worked in a hospital, and I needed help. We both took a puppy and toweled it off. As we did, she turned on the oven. I asked her what she was doing. She said she was making a makeshift incubator to warm them up. She had the temperature low, and we put the wrapped-up puppies on the rack and left the door open. The heat would warm them up, and then we could try to feed them. It took about an hour for the puppies to warm up and start to fuss.

We still didn't know if they would survive. We couldn't tell how much water was in their lungs, but they were only about three weeks old. They looked like a cross between a cocker spaniel and something else. All of them had been gold in color, very cute little puppies. I buried the dead puppies in my mother's backyard, and we focused on the two survivors.

We got out the rubber gloves, punched holes in the tips of two of them, and began them on some warm milk. We didn't have animal baby bottles in those days, but rubber gloves were easy for the puppies to wrap their little mouths around, and it worked. For several days we were seeing progress, but then another one passed away. We were left with one puppy. I left the care of this little female to my mother to take care of while I did some investigating. I contacted the person who reported the puppies in the brook. She had heard through a friend that a neighbor of hers had a female dog that got "caught" by another neighbor's dog. I ran down this information and basically hit a dead end.

The neighbor had all her puppies accounted for, and they were in good health. She then informed me that another person had Podengo dogs that he used to run rabbits, and she also heard his dog had had a litter not long ago.

She gave me his address, and I went to check it out. I had never heard of Podengo dogs, but it is a breed of dog that they raise in Portugal to run rabbit. Here in Massachusetts, it is illegal to run rabbits with dogs. First violation. The second violation is that there are no dogs licensed to this address. When I went to the address, no one was home, but I could hear a lot of barking going on. I went around the back of the house, and there was an old rabbit hutch and a lot of barking coming from it. I looked inside. Oh no!

I counted six dogs, bigger than a beagle, all stuffed inside this gross, feces-filled rabbit hutch. Third violation, no kennel license, and I bet no rabies shots. I also saw two dog bowls of, I don't know what, but they looked like bowls of puke. More grossness, if that is even a word. As I was looking at all this, a lady came out of the house, but she didn't speak English.

I gave her my name and phone number to the Police Dept and told her to have someone call me. A few hours later, I got a call from her husband and son. I told them I would come to their house and that we needed to talk. I explained to the son, who explained to his father, who also did not speak English, that he had many violations totaling lots of money and that we needed to do something right now. The son tried to explain to me that this is the way they do things in his country. I don't care! You are in America, and we have laws that need to be obeyed. First, get them out of that gross environment and get some decent dog food, not whatever that stuff is that you are feeding them. Second, they all need rabies shots and licenses, but he can only keep three. The rest have to find someplace else to live, or I will take them. That didn't go over well. Third, he cannot run rabbit with the remaining three dogs, and if I catch wind that he is, I will arrest him. Here we go again! I'm the mean person going after an old guy. I don't care about the son, the father, or the mother. My thoughts are on the dog's health and well-being. I finally had to have one of the Lieutenants who spoke Portuguese come and explain it all to them. All of a sudden, everything is fine, and they will do what they have been told to do. What, I'm a woman, and I don't speak your language, so you don't want to cooperate.

Let it go. As long as the dogs are getting better care and treatment, I'm happy. The son found and provided names and addresses for the three dogs they were not allowed to keep, and I made sure of licenses. I heard several months later that the father and son had been grabbed by Fish and Wildlife in another abutting city for running rabbits with their dogs. Some people just don't listen.

Ahh, as for the last surviving puppy from the brook, she was named Tabatha by my mother who kept her.

Horse Rescue

I got a call from a friend who I knew from the horse world asking for my help. She had been to a place in a city just outside of Boston where a guy ran a horseback riding rental place. I didn't even think they allowed horses in this city. I asked her what she wanted me to do. After all, I'm the Peabody Dog Officer, I have no jurisdiction in another city. She wanted me to come with her to this place, and maybe we could get up the $300 to buy this horse that desperately needed help. Ok, I'm a sucker for any animal being abused.

Let's take a ride and see what we have.

We took a ride to Medford. I still can't believe there is a place to ride horses here. We got there, I don't remember much about it except that it seemed out of place where it was. By that, I mean it was not in the woods or abutting woods, so where did people ride? He had a barn that had an area underneath where he kept horses. We went down into this extremely dark place.

I really could not see far in front of me. It was so dark. She says the horse is in here. I follow her in, and standing with his head down is this horse. I still can't see what he looks like, so I try the hands-on approach to see how skinny he is. I start at the neck, and I get no further than the withers, which are his front shoulders, and feel something hard and crusty.

The place was so dark I couldn't tell what this was. We take him outside. He has a lava flow of pus coming out of his withers area, obviously from many rides without a good-fitting saddle pad, which is going all the way down his side.

It actually looked like his side had split open, and this was the crusted pus coming out of it. OMG, I want to kill this man. We talked him down in price to less than $100 and a threat of a visit from the SPCA, but we got the horse out of there. We were prepared and had taken my friend's trailer with us. We loaded him on the trailer and headed back to Peabody.

This poor guy was in rough shape. While taking him back to Peabody, where we had previously arranged for a stall for him from a local farmer who was on board with helping us by providing a stall and hay for him, we called the vet and got an emergency barn call. The vet was waiting for us when we pulled in. He was shocked as well. He did a quick checkup on him and started him on some antibiotics, as this was an infection that was totally out of control. He told us that we should be prepared, that this horse might not make it.

We had a boatload of antibiotics to give him daily, and we started a warm wash to try to get the crusted pus off.

It took three buckets of warm water and antibacterial soap to get halfway through the mess. He was eating and drinking a little better but still not acting like he was getting any better. The vet came out on the third day for a recheck. The horse was still not out of the woods. His blood work was not good. The vet was starting to hear wheezing in his lungs. We just needed to keep up the antibiotics and hope.

On the fourth day, we went to the barn to find him dead. He had passed away during the night. Sometimes even the best you can do is not enough. At least he didn't die in that awful, dark, smelly underground tomb. By the way, I didn't keep my word, I called the SPCA, who already had an open complaint about the guy, and they eventually shut him down. Revenge is sweet.

Dump Dogs

Never thought we would have a wild dog problem in the dump, but we did. I got a visit from one of the local residents whose son liked to go picking through the trash for different colored bottles he made things with. Her son was only 14 but had been chased by a couple of nasty acting dogs. I haven't seen any dogs in the area around the pound. I asked the dump guys if they had seen any and they said no. We started asking some of the trash guys that came in. A couple had seen the dogs up behind the dog pound back in the woods when they were dumping loads near that area. I took a walk up in the woods with a big stick for protection.

I didn't carry a gun and didn't want to. The only gun I had was a tranquilizer gun, but I also didn't want to go unprotected. I didn't see or hear anything. A couple of weeks went by, and more calls were coming in from other people who frequented picking trash in the dump. Seems these dogs were active on days that no one was around, and they were getting more aggressive. We also had heard that there was some kind of chemical pit up in there somewhere. I didn't see it when I was up there, but I didn't go far, just in case. One person with a stick is no match for a pack of wild dogs. I had a meeting with the Chief, and he thought it best to send a couple of armed patrolmen up in the area, and if they encountered any wild dogs, they were to shoot them. The date was set, and as luck would have it, we had a rainy, cold night, so there was crunchy frost on everything. This was good because nothing could sneak up on you, you would hear the crunching of the frosty ice on the ground. I got a call that I, too, was going. Why me?

I don't have a gun, and I don't shoot animals. The Chief wanted me there. OK.

We go up into the woods, four of us, three patrolmen, and me. We are searching around and see dog prints. One of the guys finds this huge boulder, at least 7-8 ft high, and helps me get up on top of it. They don't want me following them, so they put me on top of this rock and then hand me a handgun. Really guys???? As they are walking into the woods, one calls back to me, "Look before you shoot!" I'm up high enough that no dog could possibly get to me up here, the queen of the rock, with a handgun. What a site. I'm up there a good 20-30 minutes and hear something coming from below me. I look over the edge to see a couple of puppies that have come out from under my rock, and then mum comes out. I count four puppies. I speak softly to mum, but she panics and heads back under the rock with her pups. Well, I know where they are. I have my rabies pole and crates back at my van and will need them to catch the family under the rock. I can deal with that when the guys come back. All of a sudden, I hear gunfire. Boom, boom, boom. That's a lot of gunfire. A few minutes later, more shots. I see two of the guys coming out into the path from the woods. Still, one more guy is out there hunting. As they approach, they start calling my name to make sure I don't shoot them. How cute. Don, one of the patrolmen, tells me he was walking slowly and stopped and heard crunching behind him. Seems a big dog was stalking him, and Don had just enough time to turn and shoot as the dog started to charge at him. John, the other officer, told me it took him three shots with a 30-06 to bring down the charging dog that was coming for him. He also told me the dog had a funny smell. He couldn't tell me what it smelled like, just that it was a foul smell. I told them about the mum and puppies sitting under me.

They saw the hole and, with a flashlight, saw the puppies and mum. She didn't seem aggressive, but we still had to move with caution. They went back to my van and got a large crate, big enough to hold them all, and my rabies pole. When they got back, the other officer had come back, and he, too, had a run-in with an aggressive dog, but he wasn't able to get it. He did see the chemical pit and saw paw prints around it.

One can only assume they were maybe getting into something in there that was causing the smell and the aggression.

We will never know. I wasn't dragging any bodies out of the thick woods.

We started working on getting mum and puppies out from under the rock. I thought the best way was to get the puppies into the crate, and she would go in after them to protect them. We got all the puppies in, and sure enough, mum couldn't get in there fast enough. All were safe and sound. She didn't seem to have the odor the other dogs had, according to the patrolmen. We were all trying to figure out where these dogs had come from, and the only logical explanation was that people had dumped these dogs near the dog pound, hoping I would take them in and find them homes. The problem was, I never saw them. They got together as a pack, and then the big question was, what happened? Cats can go feral very easily but not usually dogs.

Mum and puppies were taken to the vet, checked out, and deemed healthy. They needed a little human handling, and the vet techs were all on board for that job. A couple of weeks later, all were placed, and mum was fixed and also got a nice home.

Some happiness came out of a bad situation.

Snapping Turtle

A call comes into the station about a giant tortoise walking down the street. Ok, this is not Africa. We don't have tortoises. Snappers or painted turtles, that's it. A big turtle usually means a snapper, and out on the street means a female looking for a place to lay eggs. It's sad that the construction of houses has interfered with the breeding places these dinosaurs used. Then it interferes with kids and parents, who want them removed. Try to explain that they were here first. They don't want to hear it. I try to explain they are just coming out to lay eggs and then going back into the water where they came from. They still don't want to hear it. I always try to relocate away from houses, but to the same area they came from. Don't want to screw up the turtle GPS too much.

This particular time the turtle could have come from any of the local little swamps and ponds that were close by, but I had a plan in my head when heading out for the turtle.

When I got to the area, there were all kinds of folks gathered around.

Why would a snapping turtle garner this much attention? I soon found out. This was the biggest snapping turtle I ever saw. She was somewhere in the area of 20-24 inches wide, bigger than the van steering wheel. Holy smoke!

I called for a cruiser. I was going to need help. I was lucky, two cruisers showed up, but both of these guys are not animal guys, so I'll just have to get as much help as I can out of them. The turtle, who had been just sitting there resting, decided it was time to move on. I grabbed her by the tail, the only safe spot on a snapping turtle, and was holding her from moving on. I needed to get a large crate out of the van to put her in, but I was going to have to take it apart. She would never fit through the door that a big Great Dane could get through. She was just too wide. I called on the guys to come to help me. I needed one to hold the turtle by the tail while me and the other officer went to get the cage and take it apart. Richie got the tail. I told him just hold the tail to keep her from walking away and further into the bush.

Easy task. Not for Richie. While Carmen and I are getting the cage out of the truck, we hear Richie yelling for help.

I tell Carmen to just grab the cage and bring it with him while I run to see what kind of trouble Richie and the turtle are into. Well, now, it seems the turtle wanted to walk away, and she was taking Richie with her into the woods. I grabbed her tail and halted her little jaunt, and told Richie to go help Carmen take the cage apart. With the top and the door off the crate, I was able, by myself, mind you, to carefully wrestle the big lady into the bottom part of the crate, but had to tilt her sideways to do it, which is how she rode in the van, she couldn't even fit squarely in the crate she was so big, and she was so big that she couldn't turn her head to try to bite me. The ride was a short one. The guys met me down the street near a pond, and we were able to get the crate out of the van with all our limbs intact. By this time, she was in no mood for us and made that very clear.

We watched as she slowly meandered into the bush, and hopefully, she would find a nice secluded place to lay her eggs away from the general public.

Blue

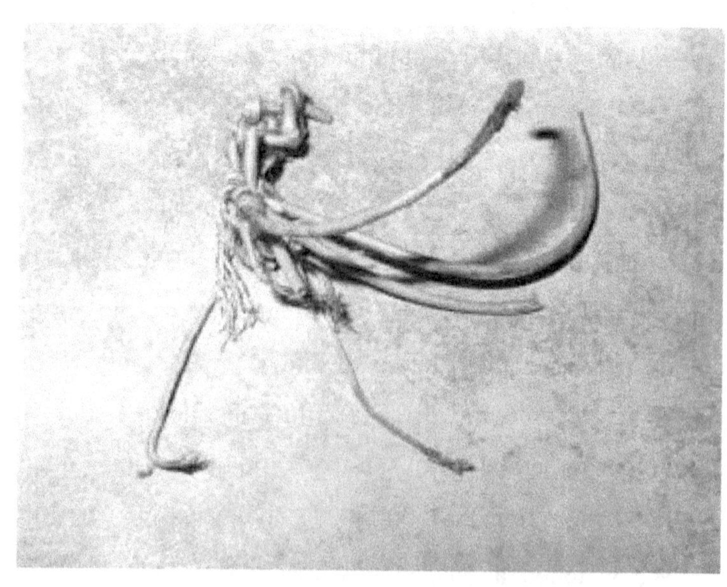

On December 5, 1985, I was called to a home on a dead-end street just outside of the center of the City. Seems a gentleman walking his pointer in the woods stumbled upon a dog. At first, he thought it was a pheasant hiding under the leaves. The dog was tied to a tree with a blue-coated clothesline, the kind the older generation used at the time to hang the laundry on.

He ran back and told his wife, who brought water and a little food for the dog, while he called for me. I got there, and here was this shepherd. Here we go again. It wasn't long ago I had the Angel cruelty case, which I wrote about in my first book. This dog was also very thin, but worse than that, the blue clothesline had dug into her neck, and it was infected and smelly and gross. I didn't need to call for the photographer this time; we could get pictures at the vet, which is where we were heading once I got her out of the woods.

I looked closer and saw that the blue-coated vinyl cord was embedded into her neck. I always carried my Swiss knife and gently cut the line off the tree.

I wasn't going to attempt to take it off her neck. I couldn't tell what damage had been caused and didn't want to cause more.

I loaded her into the van, and we took off for the vet.

I brought the dog in through the back door of the vet clinic to avoid prying eyes from people waiting in the waiting room. No need for them to see this just yet or to scare the dog. She had been through enough already. We got her weight down about 30 lbs from where it should be. She was raggedy looking, scared, hungry, thirsty, all of it, and you didn't know what you wanted to do for her first. The vet came in and started looking at her. First, we need to get this blue stuff out of her neck. It had gradually sawed its way into the skin on her throat. We didn't want to give her any sedation because we didn't want to overstress her system. We had to just be gentle and take our time. We worked slowly on this for over an hour, using warm cloths to wash down the area as we gently and slowly began pulling this out. It had a multitude of knots, obviously, this was meant to keep the dog from getting it off, and it had to be tight, maybe they were hoping she would get strangled by it. These were sick, sick people who did things like this to an animal. When we finally got this out of her neck and pulled her neck back a little to see the damage, we all gasped. There we could see the white rings of her trachea. It had sawed its way that far through the skin, muscle, and tissue. The vet said she was going to need a major debriding of the area. This means they will cut away the dead tissues, clean up the infection, insert a tube for the infection to drain, and then stitch her up. Word was traveling fast, and Blue had donations coming in to help defray the vet bills. My buddy Bill from Fish and Wildlife had heard about her and wanted to help in the investigation. We went back to the area across the street from the gentleman's house who had found Blue and I noticed his clothesline holder, one of those ones that looked like umbrellas, didn't have any rope on it. Now I could have sworn I saw clothes hanging there when I first got the call, but I'm not sure. I didn't like where my brain was going, but sometimes you just get a hunch. There were no houses close to the area Blue was found in. Behind that area is a large forested area that leads into Salem. Something just wasn't right. The man's wife was genuinely concerned about the dog, him not so much. I have no proof and can't really confront them and accuse them of what I think, so I have to let it go. Now there is another story connected to this, and you can draw your own conclusions.

About three weeks after finding Blue, the man's wife calls me and says she needs me to come to the house. She says her husband isn't home and will be back in about two hours, and she needs to talk to me and show me something. I'm thinking, here comes the truth about Blue. I couldn't have been more wrong. She is holding a box and hands it to me. I open the box to find two dead, bloody kittens. I looked up at her, and she told me that her husband beat them to death with a shovel, but she won't testify against him. She just wants the kittens to be removed and buried. I asked about Blue, and she just turned and walked away without saying a word.

I think my instincts were right.

I try to give the readers pictures of some of the cases that are not too disturbing, but when I asked a few friends what they thought of the kitten pictures, they all had the same reply, too graphic and too tough to look at. So I decided not to include them in the book.

Blue, renamed Chy by the person who adopted her, had a loving family, gained weight, and enjoyed the rest of her days as a happy dog.

I hope you have enjoyed my stories, all true, and realize that we need to do more to stop the torture of innocent animals and to educate children about the need to protect any and all creatures. They have the same feelings as you or I. The only difference is they can't tell us in a way we understand. My belief is that if you listen, they will tell you in their own way.

We also need more women and men going out in the field, whether it be in animal control, Fish and Wildlife, Border Patrol (let's kill the black market, not the animals), zoology, conservation, and so many different fields to get into to help wildlife. The world's wildlife and domestic pets need you and your support of them.

I can honestly say that in today's world, you don't see loose dogs roaming the streets anymore, people have come a long way in the responsibility of their pets, but I also know that at least 50% of the dog population of any City or Town is not licensed. People still think that a pocketbook dog or a dog that stays in the yard does not need to be licensed. Wrong folks, make it right. It's a good place to start. Get your animals chipped and up to date on shots. Volunteer, donate and do what your heart tells you to do for the sake of the animals.

This book and my first book, "Tails of a Lady Dog Catcher," are the only two books I will be writing. Thank you all for reading about my adventures.